WILDLIFE PON

How to create a natur
to attract wildlife to your garden

C000302571

CONTENTS

With thanks to Jane, Adrian, Woody and Molly

Wildflowers to create a natural looking pond

B – bog garden   E – emergent   F – floater   M – marginal   L – large ponds only

English name	Latin name	Plant Type				
		B	E	F	M	L
Amphibious bistort	Polygonum amphibium			✔		
Arrowhead	Sagittaria sagittifolia		✔			
Bogbean	Menyanthes trifoliata			✔	✔	
Brooklime	Veronica beccabunga	✔			✔	
Bugle	Ajuga reptans	✔				
Branched bur reed	Sparganium erectum	✔	✔		✔	✔
Common fleabane	Pulicaria dysenterica	✔				
Cowslip	Primula veris	✔				
Creeping Jenny	Lysimachia nummularia	✔				
Cyperus sedge	Carex pseudocyperus	✔	✔		✔	
Duckweed	Lemna minor			✔		
Devil's bit scabious	Succisa pratensis	✔				
Flowering rush	Butomus umbellatus	✔	✔		✔	
Fringed water lily	Nymphoides peltata			✔		
Frogbit	Hydrocharis morsus-ranae			✔		
Gipsywort	Lycopus europaeus	✔				
Greater burnet	Sanguisorba officinalis	✔				
Greater spearwort	Ranunculus lingua		✔		✔	✔
Hemp agrimony	Eupatorium cannabinum	✔				
Lady's smock	Cardamine pratensis	✔				
Lesser bulrush	Typha angustifolia		✔		✔	✔
Lesser spearwort	Ranunculus flammula				✔	
Marshmallow	Althaea officinalis	✔				
Marsh marigold	Caltha palustris	✔			✔	
Marsh woundwort	Stachys palustris	✔				
Meadowsweet	Filipendula ulmaria	✔				
Purple loosestrife	Lythrum salicaria	✔				
Ragged robin	Lychnis flos-cuculi	✔				
Soft rush	Juncus effusus		✔		✔	
Stiff rush	Juncus inflexus		✔		✔	
Sweet flag	Acorus calamus	✔	✔		✔	
Sweet galingale	Cyperus longus		✔		✔	✔
Valerian	Valeriana officinalis	✔				
Water avens	Geum rivale	✔				
Water betony	Scrophularia aquatica	✔			✔	
Water forget-me-not	Myosotis scorpioides	✔			✔	
Water mint	Mentha aquatica	✔			✔	
Water plantain	Alisma plantago-aquatica	✔	✔		✔	
Water soldier	Stratiotes aloides			✔		
Water violet	Hottonia palustris		✔			
White water lily	Nyphaea alba			✔		✔
Yellow flag	Iris psuedocorus	✔			✔	✔
Yellow loosestrife	Lysimachia vulgaris	✔				
Yellow water lily	Nuphar lutea			✔		✔

ONE
Introduction

The pond has always been a significant and important feature of the British landscape. Yet in the last 100 years or so, the numbers of ponds in our countryside and villages has declined by as much as a half, and with that decline much of the wildlife associated with water has also disappeared. Frogs, toads, newts and dragonflies are just a few of the more obvious creatures that we now see less often. Underneath the cool water surface a whole host of insects, molluscs and protozoa have gone for good as their habitat has disappeared.

Not so long ago every village had its pond, and every farm had several. Often constructed of puddled clay, these were important areas for the watering of animals, as well as places that played a crucial part in rural life. In the recent past the village pond and the village green were areas for recreation and getting together, where ducks were fed and people sat and talked while enjoying the wildlife round about them.

The word pond originally came from the Anglo Saxon 'pound' meaning an enclosure. A pond was a place where water was held, for use by both people and animals. Its uses were many and varied – from fire fighting when many roofs were thatched, to providing a source of food (ducks and fish) for the local population. And every village blacksmith needed water nearby. Now however, more than half of our 'natural' country ponds have been filled in, drained or sometimes polluted. Animals can be provided with fresh drinking water more easily via the mains supply, and many village ponds have been neglected or have been invaded with reeds and rushes leaving no open water as a wildlife habitat.

All this means that ponds in gardens now have a very special role where our native wildlife is concerned. They provide a breeding place for amphibians and some insects. They act as a watering hole for mammals and a place where birds can drink and bathe in safety. They provide a home for wetland wildflowers to grow and bloom.

Everyone can contribute to the conservation of our aquatic wildlife, and help our native birds, animals and wildflowers by constructing a pond, however small, in their garden. Furthermore, your pond will be the focal point of the whole garden creating fun and interest for everyone who has the time to sit and watch. This booklet is designed to get you started.

TWO
Ponds in Gardens

Having looked at the incredible importance of ponds and other wetlands in our countryside, and also at the alarming rate at which they have disappeared and are continuing to disappear, it is hardly surprising that ponds in gardens have become such vital habitats for our native wetland wildlife. Anyone who already has a garden pond will appreciate the fun and interest this feature can generate for young and old alike. As a child my family garden was never without a pond, brimming with a huge range of interesting creepy-crawlies from dragonfly nymphs and common newts to tadpoles, sticklebacks and even crayfish! As a keen angler, my father brought home a couple of these now rare native crustaceans which spent some time in our old concrete lined pond, before they were returned to their local wild habitat.

It was the wildlife in this pond that stimulated my interest and enthusiasm for natural history. I always had a selection of small creatures from the pond in a tiny aquarium in the house. It was here that I watched a male stickleback courting his female and building an underwater nest, marvelled at frighteningly ugly dragonfly larvae and learnt that water beetles could fly! The hours spent looking at drops of pond water under an old microscope opened up an even smaller and more fascinating world.

It has been estimated that around one in ten gardens has a pond of some description, but how many of them are adapted for use by wildlife? Some creatures will use them however they have been made (as long as they can get in and out of the water) but other wildlife, particularly newts and toads, may be absent. If you already have a pond of some sort but would like it to be more wildlife friendly, there is information in Chapter 7 on adapting an existing pond to encourage more varied wildlife visitors, and how to make it safer for mammals and birds. Or you may want to modify your pond to be particularly attractive to one type of creature, for instance dragonflies, or encouraging birds may be a special interest. It is possible to customise your pond in order to make it a favoured habitat for all types of wildlife visitor.

Your pond as part of the garden habitat
It is easy to look at a wildlife pond as a special feature in the garden, and of course it will be a special place for you, your family and your wildlife visitors. But to the mammals, insects, birds and amphibians that use it, it is just one part of the garden habitat as a whole. When constructing a new pond, it is important to see this special feature in relation to the other areas around it, which are vital for the survival of many of the creatures that are moving in and out of the water from one habitat to another. This means that when you design a wildlife pond, you should give some thought to the areas around it and not just plonk it down in the most convenient spot.

Chapter 3 on Pond Creation will give you some ideas about where the best place is in your garden to create a pond or other type of wetland area, but it is really important to consider the other types of habitat round about it before you start. In order to do this, we need to look at the requirements of some of the wildlife that will be using it.

A garden pond in isolation may well be used by frogs for breeding, but the young froglets, once they have legs and want to move from their watery nursery habitat to dry land, can end up as prey for many different creatures including hedgehogs, some birds and even toads. It is nature's way that many of them should be eaten and they serve as an important link in the garden food chain. If they weren't providing food for other creatures our gardens would be knee deep in frogs in no time at all! However, you do want some of them to survive to maturity to build up the frog population in your area. A garden pond surrounded by very short turf, or even that paved edging so popular in the past, has few hiding places for a small vulnerable froglet. Indeed, many young frogs can leap out of the water onto hot paving on a warm summer's day, either to be snapped up by a hungry blackbird or to be frazzled to death on the baking stones. Far better then that they can creep off into a slightly wilder habitat of long cool grass, amongst creeping plants such as bugle in a bog garden, or disappear under a pile of shady damp logs nearby.

On the other hand, your pond does need to have open and easy access for hedgehogs and foxes to safely drink, or for birds to get down to bathe without fear of cats leaping on them out of the long grass. This means that it needs a variety of different habitats around it to cover all eventualities.

The value of a pond to wildlife in part depends on its surroundings. Giving your wildlife visitors the choice of dry or damp, cool or warm conditions means that they can choose whatever they need for whichever activity is going on. So when making a decision about including a pond in your garden, it is vital that you take all these factors into account if you want to provide the best wetland habitat you can.

THREE
Pond Creation

Once you have decided that a pond is for you, first stop and think about the safety aspects. If you have young children visiting your garden you may need to think long and hard about whether a wildlife pond is the right thing for you or whether some other sort of wetland feature is a better choice, even for a limited time. If you are interested in encouraging more birds to the garden, a large terracotta saucer filled with clean water for bathing and drinking may suffice until your small human visitors are better able to cope with what could be a dangerous situation. A bird bath will not do much for your local frog population, but it will provide fresh water for birds until such time as a full blown wildlife pond is a real option. Other alternatives, such as bog gardens, mini-ponds and pebble ponds are a means of introducing water to the garden, and these are discussed in Chapter 7. If a pond is definitely for you then it may be possible to construct it in a part of the garden that can be safely and securely fenced off. Netting over a wildlife pond isn't really an option. Birds, frogs, toads and even hedgehogs can get tangled in netting, and access to the water for all wildlife is severely restricted.

Choosing the site

Once you have given due consideration to the safety aspects, and decided that a wildlife pond is for you, your next task is to choose the location. This is not as easy as you may think, as we have seen from the previous chapter just how important the surrounding habitats are. This means that you need to have space not just for the pond, but maybe for a little area of long grass somewhere beside it, or room to include a small bog garden. But don't let this put you off. Not much extra room is required - just enough to provide shelter for your emerging wildlife. And there may already be a place in the garden where your new pond can butt up to an existing 'wilder' place. However, don't neglect this requirement. The edges where habitats adjoin are very important, both in the wild and in your garden.

Next you must decide if you want the pond close to the house, to enable you to see what's happening there, or if the seclusion at the bottom of the garden is going to attract more wildlife. This is a difficult one! I have partially solved this problem by creating several ponds of varying sizes in different situations. My small pond close to the house is visible from the windows and has a steady stream of birds bathing. At night the hedgehogs are happy to drink there. It has frogs and damselflies. The larger pond in a quieter part of the garden is where the local foxes come to drink, it has a thriving population of great crested newts, and the big dragonflies such as broad bodied chasers, and emperors, breed here. We even get the occasional passing mallard! All in all it is a wilder and more exciting place. A good compromise could be a pond away from the house, and a bird drinking place outside the window. When choosing your pond location, bear in mind that access may be an issue if you intend to hire a mini digger to make the hole, although these will generally go through the average garden gate.

Lastly, don't forget that your pond will need topping up from time to time, so don't position it so far from a tap that you have a problem filling it with water. Alternatively if you can arrange for the rain water overflow from the roof of a nearby building to keep the pond topped up, you will be creating a much cleaner environment for your wildlife visitors. This can be a permanent arrangement with a hose attached to the down pipe from the guttering of a garden shed for instance, or you may wish to attach a hose to a water butt tap when you want to top up the pond. With a more permanent set-up it is quite easy to dig the hose under the soil or lawn to emerge unobtrusively in a corner of the pond.

Sun or shade?

Next look at the garden's aspect. It is always recommended that ponds are placed in full sun, but I have had greatest success with ponds in conditions where they are shaded from the sun for a part of the day, either by a fence or maybe some tall shrubs. Every new pond will have a problem with blanket weed or other types of algae when it is first constructed, but one that is in full sun all day can take longer to reach that balance where the water is clear and sparkling. A pond in a very open spot will receive lots of light and heat from the sun and this will encourage the growth of all the plant life, including blanket weed. My 'frog pond' close to the house is shaded by a group of shrubs in the morning and gets full sun only from about mid-day onwards. The water has always been beautifully clear. Similarly a mini-pond in another part of my garden that is also slightly shaded has never had a speck of blanket weed.

So does this mean that a pond can be constructed under the shade of trees? The answer is yes, but there are likely to be problems. Firstly it probably will not fulfil its main purpose which is to attract lots of wildlife. Many of the insects you may be hoping to see, especially dragonflies and damselflies prefer to be in the sunshine. Birds like to bathe in the bright morning light. Some of our most beautiful wetland wildflowers grow best in sunny conditions. Warm water is favoured by tadpoles, and attracts a wide range of aquatic insects. If you only have a very shady spot available, you can still go ahead with your pond, but it may not be a wildlife magnet. Plant ferns and other shade loving plants around it and place logs on its edges to dip down into the water. You will create a wonderfully cool, watery oasis, but don't expect quite as much in the way of visiting wildlife and do expect more in the way of maintenance.

The question of shade brings up another problem. Ponds under or near trees will undoubtedly accumulate leaves in the autumn. A few leaves falling into your pond will pose no great problem – they will sink to the bottom and help to form a layer of mud where frogs may hibernate in the winter, and flat worms, dragonfly larvae and many other creatures will live. Vast quantities of leaves falling into your pond however will break down causing a lack of oxygen in the water, to the detriment of both plants and animals. In the winter, ice may form on the pond surface and trap toxic gasses, poisoning frogs and eventually changing the ecology of your pond habitat completely. For more information on keeping your pond clean, see Chapter 6 on Pond Maintenance.

Lastly, you may have problems excavating a pond under trees if there are extensive roots. You may even damage the roots and cause problems to mature trees or the roots may puncture a flexible liner. It is obviously an area that needs a lot of thought before you start.

So where does that leave us? My choice would always be a spot that was light and open and received plenty of sunlight for much of the day, but contrary to most advice, not in the middle of a totally shade-free area. But somewhere in every garden there is a spot for even a tiny pond and don't forget that any water in the garden is better than no water at all as far as wildlife is concerned.

There is one more important consideration when you are choosing the site of your new pond. The flatter the area, the easier it will be to level the edges, making it look natural and 'at home' in its landscape. If you have a dip or hollow in the garden it may be tempting to use this, but it will not necessarily be the best spot. Sometimes an area just above the dip (as long as it can be levelled in a satisfactory way) can create a very pleasing feature, with bog plants in the lowest lying area.

What type of lining?

There are basically four types of linings for ponds, and these are outlined below, but for most situations only one is worth considering. Flexible pond liners made of butyl rubber or woven polythene are so versatile and inexpensive, there is very little reason to consider anything else, even for really large ponds, unless you have excessively stony soil. I have recently been involved in the construction and planting of a pond with a very large surface area, and a flexible liner was used to great effect, creating a large wetland habitat now full of life.

1. Concrete ponds

The pond in my parent's garden beside which I spent so much time, was made of concrete, because at that time there was no real alternative for a garden pond. Concrete however is rarely used today because of the many drawbacks associated with it. Firstly it is difficult to create a natural looking concrete pond, especially if you want grasses or other vegetation around the edges. The concrete itself may contain toxic substances which need to be locked in with a special sealant. In very cold weather, because of its rigid structure, a concrete pond can crack with the pressure of expanding ice on the surface, and be difficult to repair. All in all, concrete ponds are not particularly wildlife friendly and hard work as well.

2. Pre-formed fibreglass ponds

Most garden centres have a selection of these ponds in all shapes and sizes. Again they have their drawbacks, as the majority of them have a series of ledges around the edges to place plants, but no gently sloping side to allow easy access to wildlife. It is also not terribly easy to dig a hole exactly the right shape for the pond, which must be well supported underneath. Also, they may crack if they are full of ice in the winter. A pre-formed pond could be useful as a bird watering hole, and indeed it is now possible to get these especially for that purpose, designed to provide easy access to birds, so a small one of this type may be useful second pond near the house.

3. Puddled clay ponds

As we have already seen, the majority of our 'wild' ponds in farmyards and also our network of canals were lined with clay. It is possible to buy clay for puddling and this may be an option if you already have a heavy clay soil. However, creating a pond in this way is hard work, as the clay must be trodden with the feet to provide a smooth continuous surface to line the hole you have dug. Once a clay pond is filled with water it must never be allowed to dry out, or the clay lining may crack, and is then difficult to repair. However a puddled clay pond will look wonderfully natural, surrounded by reeds and aquatic flowering plants, and may be the choice for you. If you decide to try this method be sure to follow the manufacturer's recommendations for installation.

4. Flexible liners

The fourth option is the flexible liner, mentioned above, which can be made from a variety of substances. The most expensive and longest lasting (usually with a manufacturer's lifetime guarantee) is butyl rubber which will give you a natural looking and easy to install pond. A cheaper option is woven polythene with a life of about 30 years. Care must be taken with polythene to ensure that the edges are well covered as they may crack if exposed to sunlight for long periods.

Timing

Ponds can be created at almost any time of year, but an effective time to get going is spring. Planting up your pond is best done in April or May, so it is a good idea to have the pond ready for putting in your plants at this time. The alternative would be to do the digging and lining in the late autumn. This would allow the pond to collect some rainwater over the winter, reducing the amount of tap water needed to fill it later on. You may also find that your local wildlife starts to use this new habitat that much earlier, even if there are very few plants in it.

Designing the shape

Once you have decided on the type of liner you wish to use and the position of the pond in the garden, you need to design the shape of the pond and dig the hole.

One of the easiest ways to decide upon the outline is to use a hosepipe or length of coloured string and lay it out on the ground where you propose the pond to be. Leave it for a day or two, go back to it from time to time to adjust the shape and over a few days you will slowly see just how your new feature will fit into the existing garden. Simple shapes are best, so a gentle oval or a curved kidney shape will look most natural. However, the beauty of the flexible liner is that it can be adapted to almost any shape.

Getting started

Now you need to start digging. If you have decided to create a large pond you may need to hire some sort of mini digger. You also have to decide what you intend to do with the soil from the hole. The finished hole may look quite small but you can guarantee that the pile of soil will be enormous! If you have no obvious way of using it the best thing may be to hire a skip and remove it that way. If you are working on a relatively new garden, you may be able to distribute the soil around the new borders, but do make sure that you save some soil to go back into the pond. More of this later.

Making a meadow or creating a bank

The soil from the very bottom of the hole is ideal for creating a wildflower meadow, as it will usually be of low fertility. If you intend to create a meadow and a pond at the same time, spread some of the soil over the area where the meadow will be and allow it to settle before sowing with a seed mix in spring.

You could use the soil to create a bank of some sort in the garden and this can create a very useful wildlife habitat particularly if it is south facing. Many ponds were created in the past with a 'rockery' beside them to make use of the excess soil, but these can look terribly artificial. Instead you could sow a bank with seeds of low growing native grasses and include wildflowers such as bird's foot trefoil, speedwell or selfheal. You may wish to add a few stones or rocks here and there pushed back into the soil to create a refuge for slow worms or hibernation places for newts and toads.

Digging the hole

Start by taking off any turf if your new pond area is to be in existing grass. This can be done with a spade, or if the area is large you may want to hire a turf cutter. Put the turves to one side as they can be put to good use later.

Shapes with smooth outlines really do look best when creating a natural looking pond. The simplest shape is an oval with gently sloping sides, but it is essential to have a good proportion of deeper water to a depth of a minimum of 60 centimetres in the middle. It is best to avoid a shallow saucer shape as the large surface area will mean that evaporation and loss of water may be very rapid on hot days. The deeper you can make your central portion the better. It will provide a reservoir of cool water for the creatures that prefer these conditions and will be the best spot to plant a water lily. There will be somewhere safe for frogs (especially the males) to spend the winter, without fear of freezing and toads also seem to prefer a pond with some depth to it. A shallower pond will still be used by birds and mammals for drinking, but if you want a really good variety of wildlife try to create a deep middle section.

You can of course make the pond profile in whatever shape you wish, as long as it has at least one gently sloping side. I tend to favour a sloping edge around about one quarter to one third of the perimeter, covered with pebbles to provide safe access. A ledge of 20 to 30 centimetres depth around the rest gives a secure flat place to establish marginal plants without compromising the accessibility of the water to wildlife.

Excavate the hole to a depth of about 15 centimetres deeper all over than you expect the finished pond to be. This allows for the next stage of protecting the lining and for your planting medium to be placed on top of the liner. As you dig, try to ensure that the edges are level all round. This can be done by placing a plank of wood across the pond with a spirit level on top. If the sides are not level, you will tend to get ugly bits of exposed liner on the higher side above the water level, which can be hard to disguise with marginal plants.

Once the hole is the size and shape you want, and it will take a bit of adjusting here and there to get it right, you need to make sure that your liner is not going to get punctured by any sharp objects underneath it. Go over the soil very thoroughly and remove any bits of sharp stone, old crockery, glass or sticks that may be in the soil. To protect your liner further, line the hole with about 5 centimetres of fine sand. Other things that can be used for protection are old carpet or underlay (preferably not foam backed) old dampened newspapers, or damp cardboard. You can buy a material especially for this purpose if you have very stony soil and want to do the job really well.

Now you need to measure the hole and buy your liner. The chances are you will have already decided roughly how much liner you need, but delay ordering or buying it until you are happy with the pond shape and size. It is very easy to get carried away and create a bigger pond than you originally intended, only to find that the liner you have is too small. It is really difficult and annoying to have to fill in part of the hole you have dug.

Measuring up for the liner

There is an easy way of working out how much liner you need. Measure the length and width of the hole and then the deepest part. To calculate the length of liner you need to add twice the depth measurement to the length of your hole and then add on another metre for the overlap on the edges. Repeat this for the width – add twice the depth to the width measurement plus one metre. This will give you the length and width you need to order. Liners are available from many garden centres or by mail order and most manufacturers can provide a liner of any size by joining pieces for you if necessary.

Lining the pond

Once you are happy with the shape and size of your pond and have lined the hole with some soft material, you are ready to put in the flexible liner. Open it out carefully, get a friend to help you carry it to the hole and simply drape it over. Adjust it until you have an even overlap all the way around the hole and hold down the edges with smooth stones or bricks.

Now you have a choice. The manufacturer's instructions will probably recommend that you start to fill the pond and allow the weight of the water to gently pull the liner down into the hole. This method works well if you are not intending to back-fill the pond with soil, but a good wildlife pond should have about 10 centimetres of soil over the liner in which to grow your plants. It is easier with this type of natural looking pond to ease the liner into the hole at this stage before any water goes in, slowly releasing the stones around the edge a little at a time and gently pleating any excess liner here and there, until the liner is settled into the hole. If the pond is a simple shape, this will be very easy to do. If you want to let the liner ease down as the pond fills, you will need to throw the soil in later, which can be very messy.

Settle the liner in and then start to distribute the soil you have saved evenly over it to a depth of about 10 centimetres. Try not to walk on the liner, whatever it is made of, although butyl will take some weight. It may be easier to lie down on your stomach to spread the soil out, or simply throw it in a spade at a time. If you have made a ledge somewhere, now is the time to make use of any turf you saved. The turves turned upside down make a good planting medium for marginal plants and can be laid along the ledge with the grassy side down. The vegetation soon dies off once it is under the water. If you don't have turf, simply place a layer of soil on the ledges.

If you are making a pebble beach, now is the time to place the pebbles carefully on the slope, preferably without soil beneath them. This will ensure that the beach is kept relatively open and will not be quickly colonised by plants, ensuring easy access to the water.

When you are happy with the result you can start to fill the pond.

Filling the pond

Obviously the water in your pond is very important. Most of us have no option but to use tap water for filling, although this is not an ideal situation. If you can in any way use some stored rain water from a water butt, or you have managed to arrange for rain water to drain into the pond from a nearby roof, it will start the pond off on the right footing. Most tap water is full of things that we don't really want in a wildlife pond. The chlorine will evaporate out after a few days, but the nitrates and other nutrients are there until the plants use them up. This causes a problem - in particular it can encourage the rapid growth of algae in the first few weeks, but once you understand what is happening it need not be a issue. Chapter 4 on Planting your Pond explains how to minimize the problems caused by blanket weed and other algae.

If you are using a hose pipe, trickle the water onto a few up turned turves in the deepest part of the pond, to stop the soil layer getting too stirred up. It will look messy at first but it doesn't take long for everything to settle.

Gently fill the pond right up to the top (which may take quite some time) and then sit back and admire your handiwork. The chances are you are looking at a messy, muddy water hole with scum floating on the top! Don't worry. All ponds look like this when the water first goes in. Go away and have a cup of tea, and by the time you return there will probably be a bird or two having a drink or, as happened with the first wildlife pond I made, there may already be dragonflies hawking over the water surface, checking out this new habitat. At this point leave the pond alone for a few days to settle down.

The habitat edges

Your next job will be to work on the pond edges to create a natural looking transition between the water and the surrounding habitat. The commonest mistake with wildlife ponds is made at this point. Be aware that if you lay turf up to the edge and down into the pond, your water level will drop rapidly as water wicks up through the turf (or indeed soil) and evaporates. See the section on Bog gardens in Chapter 7 for more information on this. The art here is to have a small break at the water's edge between the soil covering the pond liner and the grass at the pond edge. This break is easier to maintain and hide with good planting if your pond has a shallow ledge. I know many people who have created the perfect looking 'natural' pond in this way, to find that it has virtually emptied overnight because of this effect.

Once you have filled your pond and created your natural looking edges, you can think about planting.

FOUR
Planting your Pond

Planting up your pond really is the fun bit. If you have completed your pond construction in spring, you can get to work planting as soon as the water has settled down, which generally takes three or four days. If your pond has been made in the autumn, it will have had plenty of time through the winter to settle down without too much input from you, but if you can get hold of plants at this stage, you can put them in straight away. Most garden centres and plant nurseries stock aquatic plants throughout the year now, but the best time to get them well established is between late March and May.

Firstly though, a word about algae. It is very common, practically normal in fact, to find that a new pond develops green water very quickly after filling. Many people get very concerned about this and attempt to put the situation right by removing some of the 'dirty' water and replacing it with clean tap water. A couple of days on and the pond is a vivid shade of green again. Alternatively, chemicals are used, which may cure the problem in the short term, but can damage plants if the amount of chemical used is not calculated accurately. A wildlife pond should be as free of chemicals as possible.

It is quite important to understand what is happening here, as understanding the processes involved will make the problem much easier to deal with. Green water contains tiny single celled algae plants which are all around us – in the water you have filled your pond with, in the soil in the garden, even in the air about us. These are tiny plants, living on nitrogen, and you have just provided the perfect conditions for their growth and multiplication. Once they are in the water in your pond, they will grow and increase until their green colour becomes visible in the form of a green soup! However, they are actually doing something very useful. They are using up the nitrates in the pond water, making a more balanced environment. Tap water in particular contains nitrates, washed into our water supply from fertilised fields, so a new pond filled with tap water will probably have a greater problem with these tiny plants than one filled with rain water. If you remove some of the water and replace it with more tap water, you are simply adding more nitrogen – feeding the plants in effect - so they will flourish afresh. All aquatic plants remove nitrogen from pond water in this way, but these tiny algae do it more efficiently than almost anything else. Once they have used up the excess nitrogen they will quickly disappear, sometimes overnight, and the water will look fresh and clear. If algal growth continues to be a problem, see Chapter 6 on Pond maintenance.

Nitrogen can get into pond water in other ways, from decomposing leaves or plants for instance, or from fish in the pond producing nitrogen in their faeces.

Keeping a balance of nutrients in the water is something we want to try to achieve. The aquatic plants you are about to add to your pond will help to set this balance up. They will clean and purify the water by using up the excess nitrogen, supply hiding places for your wildlife, shade the water surface to keep it cool and provide food for many of the creatures you hope will take up residence.

Natives or non-natives

Every wildlife pond should have plenty of wildflowers, and my own preference would be to use entirely native plants in a pond habitat. We have a wealth of beautiful wetland plants at our disposal for all areas of the pond, and this is the perfect opportunity to give some of them pride of place in your garden, but there is no harm in including one or two of your favourite non-natives if you wish. Firstly though, check that they are not plants known to cause problems if they escape into our native waterways. All plants should be chosen carefully – many will grow exceptionally quickly in these ideal conditions – and of course, they should never be taken from the wild, which is illegal. The list of wildflowers on page 2 will give you some ideas about which wildflowers are particularly suitable for garden ponds.

Sources of plants

British native plants, such as bogbean and water violet, can be found now in many garden centres in their water plant section. Unfortunately they can be rather expensive compared with plant nurseries that specialise in aquatics of this sort. Check the suppliers at the end of this booklet for an aquatic plant nursery offering an overnight mail order service.

The alternative would be to obtain bits of plant from a friend or neighbour (but it is always useful to be absolutely sure that you know what you are getting), and the advantage of this is that you will inevitably get some aquatic creepy crawlies into the bargain. As most pond plants grow quickly, we all need to thin them out from time to time and they generally go straight onto the compost heap. I would much rather pass these onto a friend starting up a new pond if I can. Oxygenators in particular can grow exceptionally quickly, and these usually have the eggs of water snails on them, or small damselfly larvae clinging to the leaves.

Types of plants

Of all the types of plant we can grow in our gardens, pond plants are about the most rewarding. In the right conditions they will grow quickly and make your pond look mature and inviting within a few months. Many also have the advantage of adapting to wet soil, or they will grow in several centimetres of water on the pond ledge. In general though, pond plants are divided into several different categories, and a well-stocked pond will have a few of each type.

1. Emergents

These are very important plants in the pond, as they are rooted well below water level, and have their leaves above water level. This means they are available for creatures such as dragonfly larvae to easily leave their watery habitat when they are ready to transform into beautiful winged insects. The larvae will crawl up the plant's leaves (even easier if the leaves are smooth and sword shaped) into the air, where they will complete their transformation. Good examples of emergent plants are all the rushes and sedges, branched bur reed, flowering rush and yellow flag or iris. Emergents usually adapt to the pond ledge or areas of the pond where the water is relatively shallow.

2. Floaters

Plants with floating leaves are important to provide shade on the water during warm, sunny weather. They will help to keep the pond cool and prevent the spread of blanket weed and other algae. Any plant with floating leaves, however small, will perform this function, but water lilies are our most useful ally in shading the water. This is a good opportunity to use a non-native plant if you wish. The native white water lily is a large plant, not really suitable for a small pond, so choose a smaller non-native if you would like a lily. Other good shading plants are fringed water lily, duckweed and frogbit. Aim to have at least 30 per cent of the water surface covered with leaves in the summer. Floaters such as lilies are generally planted into the deepest part of the pond.

3. Marginals

These are the really adaptable plants which will often grow in damp soil as well as on the pond ledge. They provide a very important habitat for wildlife around the margins of the pond as well as giving it a natural look by hiding the liner when the water level drops. Many of our native wetland plants are marginals and include such colourful species as water mint, brooklime, spearwort, and marsh marigold. Some marginals can also be classed as emergents (yellow flag for example) and many will also grow in boggy conditions.

4. Oxygenators

These are crucial in your new pond as they provide the oxygen upon which your pond wildlife depends. If you can possibly find a source of native oxygenators, then do use them. They will generally grow less quickly than non-natives, which can be very invasive. They will also provide a better home for the small aquatic creatures that will find their way into your pond. However, if only non-natives are available to you make do with them. Oxygenating plants are vital in a pond, which will not thrive and achieve a balance without them. But choose carefully, and make sure that you avoid the really invasive species listed on page 18. Oxygenators should be placed in the deeper water.

Cool water shaded with arrowhead and water lilies

A green oasis in a wildlife garden

A mini-pond in a half barrel is a good
wildlife habitat in a small garden

Refuge on the
pond edges is
important

Marsh marigold on a pond margin

Bugle, snakeshead fritillary,
ragged robin and
meadowsweet - four
wildflowers for bog gardens

A pond in winter needs regular attention to keep some open water

A pebble dish for birds to drink

Dragonflies hunt from a vantage point

A wildlife pond can be a source of interest in the garden at any time of year

Adult frogs are happy both in and out of water

A newly emerged emperor dragonfly

A Libellula dragonfly

5. Bog plants

In general bog plants are species which prefer a soil that never dries out completely and include some of our most colourful wildflowers. Purple loosestrife, ragged robin, bugle and lady's smock are all good examples. If you are not planning a separate bog garden, you may be able to include some of these species around the pond margins. Be aware, though that the edges of artificial ponds can actually be very dry and the ledge itself may be too wet. A gently sloping edge may be the best spot for some bog loving species which will adapt and find their preferred water depth by self seeding or spreading by runners. Don't forget though to keep some of your gentle slope completely free of plants.

Inevitably, all these different types of water plant will seed and spread all around the pond until they find a place where they are happy, but it is a good idea to at least start off with a few of each kind.

How to plant

One of the special features of a wildlife pond is its natural look and this is achieved by planting your aquatic plants directly into the soil covering your liner rather than in containers. If you have placed inverted turf on a pond ledge, this is a perfect planting medium for marginals and emergents. The general idea though is to take the plants out of their pots (if they have them) and push the whole rootball into the mud or turf. Some plants may want to float back up to the surface at this point. If so, anchor them down with a large stone propped onto the rootball – it can be removed when the plant has established a root system in the mud, which happens very quickly. Plants such as lilies for deeper water should be carefully removed from the pot or planting basket they arrive in, and the rootball wrapped in a piece of hessian. Tie the hessian gently around the plant stem to keep the whole thing together and then carefully throw the plant into the deepest area of water. I have never found it necessary to lower lilies into the water to allow the leaf stems extend to over a few days. They always seem to have survived this rather brutal introduction to their new home! If however you are creating your pond in spring time, you may prefer to place the lilies in position as the pond is being filled.

This natural way of planting up your pond will give you lots of vegetation for pond wildlife to live and thrive. However there are some plants that are just too vigorous for small garden ponds, and should be planted with caution. They could however be introduced to your pond in conventional planting baskets, but bear in mind that plants can escape from baskets over time. These plants are marked as suitable for very large ponds only in the table on page 2.

Oxygenators also need to be planted – only a few survive by floating around in the water. Push the cut or rooted ends into the soil in the deepest water you can safely reach, or add them to the pond soil as it is filling with water. Where possible try to get native oxygenators. Listed below are a few that are sometimes available from specialist nurseries:

Native oxygenators

Curly pondweed	Potamogeton crispus
Hornwort	Ceratophyllum demersum
Spiked water milfoil	Myriophyllum spicatum
Water starwort	Callitriche ssp.

If natives are not available Canadian pondweed (Elodea canadensis) is a good oxygenator and can usually be kept under control, but make sure it does not 'escape' into natural aquatic habitats.

Avoid at all costs!
There are a few non-native plants (particularly oxygenators) that are causing enormous ecological problems in our native wetland areas. These have generally escaped from garden ponds, or have been dumped by unsuspecting gardeners, not knowing what problems they are causing. They are dangerously invasive, threatening these precious natural habitats. Do not plant the following under any circumstances:

Non-native plants to avoid

Alien marsh pennywort	Hydrocotyle ranunculoides
Curly waterweed	Lagarosiphon major
New Zealand stonecrop	Crassula helmsii (Tillaea recurva)
Nutall's pondweed	Elodea nutallii
Parrots feather	Myriophyllum aquaticum
Water fern	Azolla filiculoides

If you have any of these plants in an existing pond, contact your local Wildlife Trust for advice about disposing of them. NEVER dump them in the countryside, particularly not in wetland habitats. Most plants will break down naturally on the compost heap, especially if they are chopped up first. Hopefully these plants will soon no longer be found for sale in nurseries and garden centres.

FIVE
Pond Wildlife

Perhaps the most exciting thing about a wildlife pond is that you hardly need to do anything except add water to attract at least some wildlife. Dragonflies, water beetles, water boatmen, pond skaters – many fascinating creatures will investigate a new pond without plants on day one if they get the chance. Plant up your pond thoughtfully though, and a huge range of aquatic life will make use of the water to live and breed, or simply to drink and bathe. And you don't have to introduce your wildlife – everything will find your new habitat by itself.

We have seen how important the construction of the pond can be, especially in terms of access to wildlife. If you already have a garden pond that is not particularly wildlife friendly in terms of easy access to the water, Chapter 7 has some ideas on adapting an existing pond to make it a better habitat for wildlife.

To a certain extent, the size, shape and depth of your new pond will determine the type of creatures that will use it, as will the habitat around it. But the average garden pond is quite capable of attracting frogs and common newts, several species of dragonfly and damselfly, water snails, boatmen, beetles and pond skaters as well as many other smaller aquatic insects. Birds of all shapes and sizes will visit even a tiny pond – my average sized garden pond regularly has a couple of mallard visiting on quiet evenings. Hedgehogs and foxes will drink from the smallest saucer pond. So what wildlife can we reasonably expect in an average garden pond?

Amphibians

Frogs, toads and newts use our ponds for breeding in springtime but spend much of the rest of the year in the surrounding habitat – hence the importance of getting that right when your pond is constructed. Spawning can begin as early as January (frogs) in the south, toads spawn a little later in March or April and newts latest of all (April or May).

Frogs are the most common of the amphibians to use garden ponds – indeed there are thought to be more common frogs in suburban areas now than in the countryside. They are not particularly fussy about the type of pond they use, and generally lay their jelly-like blobs of spawn in shallow water at the pond edge. Toads lay their spawn in long strings like transparent necklaces with the black eggs visible along the length, and they wind the spawn around aquatic plants. In general toads prefer a pond with a good deep area, and sometimes frogs and toads won't co-habitat in the same pond. Common or smooth newts may find their way into even the smallest pond. They lay single eggs which they attach to the undersides of plant leaves, especially oxygenators. The eggs are usually

19

very difficult to see. Great crested newts will also use a garden pond, but this rare amphibian does not occur in many places in Britain and is a protected species. In the Thames Valley area where I live, it is relatively common and my wildlife pond has a good population of these beautiful and fascinating amphibians. Great crested newts are almost black and extremely large – up to 18 centimetres in length - so they can be distinguished by size and colour from common (also called smooth) newts which are usually muddy brown. Great crested newts are fully protected by law under the Wildlife and Countryside Act 1981 and their habitat should not be disturbed in any way. If they are common in your area they will happily co-habit with smooth newts, but remember that they will eat frog spawn and tadpoles, which may deplete your population of these amphibians.

Lastly, beware of importing frogspawn from other ponds – it is an easy way to spread disease.

Reptiles
The only native reptile likely to use a garden pond is the grass snake. They are particularly attracted to water, love to swim, and frogs make up a major part of their diet. Again they are a protected species and the habitat around your pond will be important if you want to attract this reptile. Compost heaps are favourite breeding places.

Larger insects
Many insects breed in water and the dragonflies and damselflies are favourites with many people. The size of the pond is significant when attracting these insects, as the larger species of dragonfly, especially the beautiful green emperor, prefer a big pond. The larvae may spend many months in the water, depending on the species, and they feed on the smaller creatures in the silt layers at the bottom of the water. They are all dependent on the surrounding habitat as, like the aquatic larvae, the adults also live on the smaller insects they can hunt and catch around the pond. Your pond plants on the water margins are also important as these enable the larvae to emerge when they are ready to leave the water in spring and early summer. In our countryside, many of our native dragonfly and damselfly species are declining due to destruction of habitat, so garden ponds can be havens for the smaller species.

Water boatman, water beetles and pond skaters are some of the more visible insects that inhabit a garden pond. Many people have concerns about the larvae of mosquitoes, midges or gnats that breed in water, but in general these are never a problem in a well-balanced pond. The vast majority will provide food for frog and newt tadpoles or other carnivorous insects such as the great diving beetle, which can even catch and eat small fish!

Smaller creepy crawlies

A well-balanced pond will soon accumulate a wide range of the smaller creepy crawlies that inhabit water at some point during their life cycles. All have important roles in a wildlife pond. Daphnia, water fleas or mites for example, provide food for the larger creatures and water snails are important for keeping the water clean and fresh. Encourage all that comes, as it will have its place in the overall scheme of things and in the food chain in the garden as a whole. Swallows, swift and martins, as well as bats rely on the small winged insects that hatch from the pond over the summer months. To find out more about the smaller creatures and the roles they perform, get a good identification book on the subject and indulge in a bit of pond dipping.

Mammals

We have mentioned the importance of water to mammals that come to the garden. Hedgehogs and foxes in particular will drink at a wildlife pond, provided the access is easy and safe, and in my garden muntjac and roe deer are occasional visitors.

Birds

All birds need to bathe and drink — finches in particular have a very dry diet, eating mainly seeds, and seem to need to visit fresh water regularly. Goldfinches, greenfinches and linnets are frequent and very welcome visitors in my garden. If you have chosen to provide a bird drinking dish rather than a full blown wildlife pond you can still expect a very wide range of birds of all shapes and sizes.

Occasionally herons are a problem, but usually only in ponds stocked with fish. Herons will also eat frogs and toads so do expect to see them from time to time, even if your pond is small. If they really are eating everything in your new habitat, do not be tempted to place a plastic heron beside the pond to deter the real thing. This is more likely to encourage a friend for your pretend bird! Herons are quite often seen fishing in groups — the sight of a 'bird' at your pond edge may well make a real heron think there is food available. The best deterrent is a thin strand of wire about 20 centimetres high around the edge of the pond. Herons tend at alight at the pond edge and then walk into the shallow water. A strand of wire deters them when they brush it with their legs. Alternatively, try to appreciate this graceful native bird and make sure that your frogs and toads have plenty of cover.

Fish

In general, fish and wildlife ponds do not mix. Koy carp or goldfish are better off in pond of their own, as they will quickly devour spawn or tadpoles, thus preventing the build up of a population of these amphibians. They also excrete nitrogen into the water which can aggravate a blanket weed problem. If you really would enjoy fish in your pond, sticklebacks are fascinating and can breed well in garden ponds, but they are very aggressive little fish and their diet consists of many of the other small creatures you are providing a home for.

Wildlife and the Law
Lastly a word on the law and aquatic wildlife. We have seen how some species, especially great crested newts and grass snakes, have special protection in law because of their decline over the last few years. There is legislation governing the introduction of many species to garden ponds, and handling some plants or amphibians may require a licence. Similarly the release of plants or animals (especially exotic species such as terrapins or bullfrogs) in an unauthorized place is against the law. If you are in any doubt about these issues, contact your local Wildlife Trust, or the Environment Agency.

SIX
Pond Maintenance

Taking care of your pond to maximise its wildlife potential and keep it looking attractive and healthy is something that requires a gentle touch. After construction, it would be possible to do nothing at all and to create a wonderful wildlife paradise for a couple of years. But doing nothing means that the pond habitat will slowly change as it evolves naturally into a bog. This could still be a useful wildlife habitat, but is not what we are trying to achieve in a garden situation. On the other hand, a pond that is continually cleaned, disturbed and interfered with may look sparkling and pretty, but will probably not be home to lots of species that prefer a bit of privacy.

The answer here is to do as little as possible while still maintaining a habitat with plenty of open water between a good covering of plants. Below are some of the maintenance jobs that may need to be done on a seasonal basis.

Spring and summer
These are the seasons to leave things alone as much as possible. It is sometimes suggested that excess duckweed is removed from a pond in the springtime, but this is when floating plants are particularly valuable as a means of keeping frog and toad tadpoles safe from predators. Only remove plants at this time if they are particularly overgrown and threatening to close up all the open water, and even then do this using extreme caution. Remember that newt eggs are laid individually onto the leaves of oxygenators and other plants, so try not to thin these out at all at this time.

Throughout spring and summer make sure that your pond is topped up little and often. If you have been able to arrange the rainwater overflow from a roof or a water butt to flow into the pond, this may be only an occasional job, depending on the weather. If you are relying on tap water, a little now and again will help to avoid the problem of great quantities of nitrates entering the habitat in one go.

If blanket weed is a problem at this time, try adding a bundle of barley straw which is thought to produce a natural compound that inhibits the growth of algae. Check carefully the proprietary products in garden centres as some of these are impregnated with a chemical algicide.

Autumn
Autumn is the time to remove excessive plant growth, but it should still be done with extreme care. By the autumn the larger animals - frogs, newts and toads - will have left the water. Frogs, particularly the males, may return to hibernate in the mud at the bottom of your pond as the weather gets colder so if you are doing any cleaning work, October is a good month to choose. Plants such as

duckweed and oxygenating plants can be removed gently with a rake. Take great care not to scrape the bottom of your pond! Liners can be easily damaged, and although they are repairable, there is nothing worse than finding your pond empty the day after a clean-out (as I have), and it could take a long time for the wildlife to recover.

Any plants removed in this way should be left overnight or longer on the pond side to allow the aquatic creatures in them to crawl out back into the water. You will be amazed at the number of small dragonfly and damselfly larvae, water snails and freshwater shrimps living in this vegetation. You can help the process if you wish by sorting through the plants and collecting the larvae and other things you find, but in general it is easier to allow them to find their own way back into your pond. Once you are fairly sure there is nothing left, these excess plants can be put on the compost heap, or better still, passed onto a friend setting up a new pond.

Usually it is only rapidly growing plants such as oxygenators that need this treatment, but every couple of years you may need to reduce the volume of some of the marginals and deeper water plants. If you have been careful not to plant the really rampant species mentioned in Chapter 4 and on page 2 you should be able to do this without creating too much disturbance. Plants such as fringed water lily, water mint and bogbean will have spread by runners and can generally be uprooted from the mud at the bottom of the pond fairly easily. Others like cyperus sedge, purple loosestrife or gipsywort may seed too freely in shallow water, and will need to be loosened from the mud and removed to the compost heap. Any plants in containers can also be dealt with at this time of year. Lift the container from the water, gently dislodge the plant and split the root by hand or with a sharp knife. Repot the section you want to retain, covering the soil around the plant roots with a layer of gravel to prevent the compost from floating out when the container goes back into the water.

The other important autumn task is the removal of excessive quantities of leaves from the pond. A few falling into your pond will not matter hugely, but large quantities will break down and increase the nutrient levels, causing problems later with the growth of blanket weed and other species of algae. Leaves can also cause a problem as they decompose over the winter months. They may produce toxic gasses such as methane during their decomposition. This, when trapped under a frozen pond surface, may affect the survival of frogs and other creatures spending the winter months in the depths of the pond. If you have large quantities of leaves in your garden they should be gently raked from the pond surface on a regular basis through the autumn. Netting a pond to catch leaves is not a good option, as many creatures can become entangled or trapped.

Winter
During the winter months, your pond may look lifeless, but a great many creatures are resting under the water surface and your concern at this time is to ensure

that they survive the cold weather. If you have constructed the pond with a depth of at least 60 centimetres, most creatures will be safely pass the winter months in the deepest past of the pond, but a covering of ice may affect their chances of survival. The safest and most effective way of clearing a 'breathing hole' for your pond is by using a small metal saucepan of very hot water. Simply hold the base of the saucepan on the ice surface, and let the heat slowly melt a circle of ice. This will effectively open up a space, allowing gasses to escape, without greatly disturbing the wildlife beneath the surface. It is not advisable to pour hot water onto the ice, or to break a hole in it. Both these actions are thought to produce a 'shock' effect in the water, which may be detrimental to the wildlife there.

Repairing leaks

Most flexible pond liners can be repaired, using a kit from the manufacturer or garden centre. These are very effective, but do rely on the liner surface being completely dry. If your liner has been torn, either by careless use of a rake, or some other accidental damage, allow the water to leak out until it maintains its level. The hole will be somewhere on this level. It will then be necessary to manually remove a little more water until the tear is completely exposed and can be effectively dried. Follow the repair kit instructions and be prepared to repeat the operation! It generally works in the end, but not necessarily first time. If your pond has sprung a leak halfway down or more, try to repair it as soon as possible regardless of the time of year. A pond that empties due to a tear in the liner will be of little use to the wildlife living there if the water disappears completely. If the leak is nearer the surface, try to keep the pond well topped up until the autumn which is the best time for repair.

Removing a build up of silt

Again choose the autumn for this job. If your pond has accumulated so much silt that the depth of water is greatly reduced, it will be necessary to remove some of it. You may decide to take out some of the water, or to attempt the job, particularly if your pond is small, by leaning in and scooping out some of the sludge with a smooth edged receptacle such as a plastic food container. Equip yourself with a large sheet of polythene, spread out at the pond side, and begin by heaping up the surface layer of silt here. This can be reintroduced to the pond (it will contain vast numbers of useful creepy crawlies and bacteria) once the sludge from the very bottom has been taken out and put on the compost heap. However you perform this messy task, keep all sharp tools away from the pond liner!

Renovating your pond completely

This is a job to avoid at all costs if you can. By cleaning out a pond completely you could be destroying a habitat that has been built up over many months or years. Keeping your pond maintained at a low but continuous level throughout its life could avoid such drastic action. If you have great crested newts in your pond you will be breaking the law to cause such disturbance.

If you are sure you do not have newts, and need for whatever reason to reconstruct your pond, you must have an alternative nearby to hold the creatures you will find. Fill an old bath or other container with water from the pond (not fresh tap water), add as many plants, particularly oxygenators, as you can and carefully transfer any creatures as you find them. Return them to the new or refurbished pond, as soon as you can.

Maintenance of the area around your pond.

We have already seen how the habitat around your pond is of great importance. Take great care when mowing long grass near a pond, and avoid disturbance of log piles and other areas when you are carrying out work nearby. There may be newts, toads, even grass snakes residing there. Long grass near a pond could be carefully cut on a rotational basis, ensuring that there is always somewhere for your wildlife to live in safety.

By and large, try to do a little regular pond maintenance every autumn, rather than leave the jobs to pile up. The less disturbance you create in your habitat, the happier your wildlife will be.

SEVEN
Pond Alternatives

We have already seen from Chapter 5 how important any water is in the garden to your visiting wildlife. Many creatures would not be your garden at all if it wasn't for their daily visit to the drinking water you are providing. Others such as frogs, toads, newts, dragonflies and damselflies rely on water for breeding and thus maintaining their populations. Many smaller creatures live their whole lives in water, and we have seen that by providing a source of water you are contributing to the conservation of many species that are declining in the countryside. But a pond is not for all of us for a variety of reasons. We must therefore look at alternative ways of providing water for wildlife for people with small children, or those with little space or with no time to carry out maintenance.

Starting small
Even on a patio or tiny roof garden we can provide clean drinking water for birds and mammals such as hedgehogs (although a roof garden may be a bit beyond the latter!) A terracotta plant saucer, perhaps with a few smooth pebbles to make it attractive, will be gratefully used by your local bird population for drinking and bathing. Placed in a sunny spot, there will be a constant stream of blackbirds and house sparrows washing their feathers and greenfinches will come to drink at frequent intervals. A saucer of this sort, outside my back door, has attracted around 10 species of bird, and provides a fascinating sight at almost any time of day. The alternative to this is to provide one of the purpose built bird drinking and bathing dishes available from many of the bird food suppliers, or the RSPB. Your only commitment is to ensure that it is topped up with fresh water every day, cleaned out thoroughly from time to time, and de-iced in cold weather. Position your pebble dish in an open area, to ensure that any cats around have nowhere to hide and spring an ambush.

The alternative to a pebble dish is a birdbath. These seem to have gone out of fashion, but can be extremely useful where birds are concerned and have the added advantage of being relatively safe from cats. Look out for the type that can be attached to a fence or post if you are short of space.

A water feature
The current trend for elaborate water features would seem to have little to do with wildlife gardening, but there is a case for the notion that any water in the garden is better than no water at all, as long as it is accessible to wildlife. On a recent visit to a large garden in North Devon, I was amazed to see a robin repeatedly visiting a water feature in full view of many members of the public. The feature consisted of a large stone with a hole through the middle, up which

water was pumped to give a pleasant trickling sound. The robin sat in the bubbling water on top of the stone, fluffing up his feathers and enjoying a bath! If you intend to install something of this sort in your garden, try to make sure that birds at least have access to the water. But be aware that anything with steep sides will not provide good access, and could be a problem for many species.

A mini-pond

Whilst the alternatives above will have some value for birds and possibly hedgehogs in your garden, they will do nothing for the insects or amphibians that rely on water. However a mini-pond constructed in a half barrel or similar small container will often provide a home for a few frogs and common newts, as well as some of the smaller species of damselfly.

Half barrels are often available from garden centres, but may have holes drilled in the bottom for use as planters. Not much good for a pond! If you can get one without holes, you will find that it generally holds water quite well – after all its previous use may have been as a container for rum or cider. If it has been allowed to dry out, and will not hold water, it will need to be soaked in a large container full of water. Alternatively, make sure it is left out in wet weather and fill it up daily, until the wood is wet through and it holds water. Once this happens, you will need to ensure that it is always topped up. If it is allowed to dry out, you will need to go through this process again.

A mini barrel or container pond can be placed on a patio in full view of the house, or sunk into the ground in an out of the way spot. Make sure it is in its final position before you plant it up and add water. As these barrels have straight sides, it is necessary to make them more wildlife friendly, particularly if you are hoping for frogs or newts to use them. Those sunk into the ground are much more likely to attract these amphibians. Begin by placing a layer of soil, to a depth of about 10 centimetres or so in the bottom of the barrel, as a planting medium for your aquatic plants. Cover this with a thin layer of gravel or pea shingle if you wish. Next, along one side, place a narrow layer of turf, upside-down, to create a platform level with the water surface. If your pond has been sunk into the ground, this will allow frogs and newts to get in and out safely, and create a ledge for birds to bathe and drink from. It will also provide a planting place for marginals. The pond can be filled with rain water or tap water at this point and allowed to settle down for a day or two.

Planting is the next task and must be thought through carefully. The last thing you need in such a small habitat is anything invasive, but it is still important to have plants from all the categories mentioned in Chapter 4. Below are some suggestions of useful wildflowers for mini-ponds of this type.

Wild plants for mini-ponds

Emergents	Soft rush, lesser spearwort
Floaters	Fringed water lily, duckweed, frogbit
Marginals	Brooklime, lesser spearwort, water mint
Oxygenators	Curly pondweed, hornwort, water milfoil

To introduce your chosen plants, simply push the roots of the oxygenators and fringed water lily into the layer of soil beneath the gravel. Emergents such as soft rush, and your chosen marginals can have their roots tucked into the turf ledge. Frogbit and duckweed simply float decoratively on the water surface. The objective with your plants is to have a varied and attractive mix – spiky rushes contrasting with flat leaved floaters and colourful flowering marginals.

None of these is very invasive, and a pond of this size is quite easy to maintain. Taking out excess plant growth in the autumn every year will be enough to keep your mini-pond looking good. Try to keep about two thirds of the surface water open and plant free.

If you prefer to include some non-natives, ensure that they are small and slow growing, or your mini-pond will be taken over in one season. The small species of bulrush (Typha minima) is lovely and non-invasive, and you may like the white flowered variety of our native marsh marigold.

As we have already seen, a barrel pond like this will provide a small watery habitat for quite a range of aquatic wildlife as well as a place where birds will drink and bathe. However, if the pond is on a patio, rather than sunk into the ground, there will be restricted access for creatures such as frogs and newts unless you also construct a ramp of some sort at one side. This can be done, but it is generally better to assume that a patio barrel will encourage birds and damselflies, water boatmen and water beetles, rather than amphibians.

Bog gardens

Bog gardens are wetland habitats of a sort, but generally they do not have open water. Often they are constructed alongside a pond, using any overflow of pond water to maintain the dampness that the plants require. They have a limited value to the aquatic wildlife in your garden, but can be useful places for growing wild marsh plants, most of which provide nectar or pollen for insects. A bog garden is, however, a useful refuge for small frogs, toads and newts emerging from your pond, providing them with sheltered hiding places when they are most vulnerable. Some species of dragonfly and damselfly will lay their eggs on plants near to open water, so a bog garden can be useful in this respect, too.

Bog garden construction, in order to grow exotic Primulas or Hostas, can be a complicated affair, but for the purpose of providing an additional habitat for wildlife, we can simplify construction considerably. All that is needed here is a place where water does not drain away quickly, and supports plants that require a wet soil. However, the danger of a simple construction is that the soil in an area such as this can become stagnant and unhealthy. It is not enough simply to fill a hole with an old piece of pond liner and introduce marsh plants – some drainage is needed to ensure a flow of water through the area to keep the soil aerated and fragrant! This flow of water, however slow, can create a problem when a pond is constructed with a bog garden attached, as water may drain from one to the other surprisingly quickly. I would always construct a boggy patch as a completely separate area, even if it is alongside a wildlife pond. Where open water and soil are connected, it is possible for water to wick out of the pond and evaporate, causing the water level in the pond to fall very rapidly, and we have seen in Chapter 3.

Bog garden construction begins with digging a suitable hole, which can be alongside your pond, where it will provide a welcome additional habitat for wildlife, or it can be elsewhere in the garden if you prefer. Areas in full sun or part shade are suitable, but be aware that a bog garden in full sun is likely to dry out more quickly and will require more frequent topping up to keep the plants happy. The depth needs to be between 30 and 60 centimetres and lined with what ever you have available – an old piece of pond liner will work well, or sturdy plastic of some sort. The bog will need drainage as already mentioned, so once the liner is in place, spike it with a fork across the bottom, to enable water to drain out slowly. If you wish you can now place a layer of gravel in the bottom, to aid drainage further, but if your intention is to grow wildflowers such as purple loosestrife and ragged robin, this is not really necessary.

Start to backfill the hole with your garden soil, adding a little home made compost or leaf mould if you have any as this will help to hold water. Avoid something as rich as farmyard manure, as, if you intend to grow wildflowers, you may find the rich soil reduces the numbers of flowers at the expense of the foliage. At about the halfway point you may want to consider introducing a length of pipe, attached to an overflow from a nearby water butt. If there is no overflow facility, one can be easily made by drilling a hole near the top of the butt, and fitting the end of a piece of hose pipe tightly into it. Dig the pipe into the ground, allowing the other end to come to rest inside the bog garden. Once it is in position, arrange a few stones around the open end, to prevent it from becoming blocked with soil. Whenever your water butt is full, the overflow will now top up your bog garden with fresh clean rainwater. Now continue to fill the bog garden with soil until the liner is completely covered.

The bog garden can now be planted with your favourite wetland plants. See the table on page 2 for a few suggestions.

Adapting an existing pond

Inherited ponds can be a bonus in a new garden. However, we are much more wildlife friendly in our gardens now than in the past, and many older gardens have ponds made of concrete with straight, steep sides. This makes them very unsuitable for wildlife. They may well have frogs or newts finding their way in or out, but from a bird's eye view, these ponds can be hazardous to say the least. It is very distressing to find a drowned bird in a garden pond, which fell in whilst drinking and was unable to scramble out. Even worse is the sight of a dead hedgehog that has slipped in overnight. Hedgehogs are good swimmers, but if there is no obvious exit, they can tire and drown quite easily.

Straight-sided ponds can be adapted in a variety of ways. The simplest way, if the pond is not too deep, is to build up one corner with stones, soil and turf to water surface level and plant wildlife friendly marginals. If the pond is too formal for this adaptation, and you wish to preserve the formality, a series of planting baskets with irises or other wetland plants can also provide a platform for birds to use safely, as long as they are near the water's edge. They will also create a lifeline for a hedgehog that may have fallen in, and an easy access point for frogs and newts.

If the pond is exceptionally deep, the only answer may be to provide a ramp of wood, weighted down on the bottom of the pond with stones or bricks. Try to arrange that the other end reaches the bank amongst thick planting.

If none of these remedies is appropriate, try to provide another small pond in the garden, that is safe for wildlife, and give your visitors a choice. They will certainly use the easier option for access to water.

In Conclusion

Almost everyone with a patch of garden can provide water for our native wildlife. Whether it's a large wetland habitat or a mini barrel pond, you will be creating a wonderful and important resource for all the wildlife around you that requires water for breeding, bathing or simply to drink. And don't underestimate the huge amount of pleasure you will get from seeing this wildlife close at hand. Hopefully you are now preparing to create a wildlife pond somewhere in your garden and will soon find out for yourself just what an exciting habitat this can be.

NOTES